Growing Up Like Joseph

Copyright © 2017 by Nadirah M. Muhammad

Printed in the United States of America

All rights reserved . No part of this book maybe reproduced, distributed, or transmitted in any form or by any means, including photocopying, recording, or other electronic or mechanical methods, without the prior written permission of the publisher, except in the case of brief quotations embodied in critical reviews and certain other noncommercial uses permitted by copyright law. For permission requests, write to the publisher, addressed "Attention: Permissions Coordinator," at the email address below.

giftedfamilyinstitute@gmail.com or nadirah@nadirahmuhammad.com

Edited by: Karen Cioffi

Illustrated by: Janine Carrington

First Printing, 2017

ISBN: 978-0-692-05442-0

Acknowledgements

"We took our eye off the prize. What is the prize? It is our children. Our children are our future. Our children is where our heart should be. Our children should be the number one priority of leadership today-Saving Our Youth."
— The Honorable Minister Louis Farrakhan, The Time and What Must Be Done, 'We Must Unite to Save Our Youth,'
Part 23

I am forever grateful to Almighty God, Allah for granting me the idea for my first book, bringing it to fruition with the help of others in my life, and guiding me along the path
to publication. The Honorable Minister Louis Farrakhan also had a hand in creating this book, as his powerful words in "Looking at Family from the Perspective of Children" inspired me to finally take action. His words further inspired my next books, a series
that will look at various experiences from the perspective of a child.
The goal of this series is to allow an opening for the child's voice in the midst of the cacophony that exists in many families' homes, and also remind parents that all children have a need and right to feel secure and safe as they grow up.

The Collaborative Therapeutic approach is much appreciated and integrated into this book, as it emphasizes valuing, respecting, and validating all perspectives, and viewing the client as the expert in their own life.

I cannot convey my gratitude to my three adult children enough—they helped come up with the title of this book and have my deepest thanks and love.
It wasn't until my middle child mentioned during a brainstorming session that he was Joseph that it occurred to me the impact the divorce had on him still. As a mother, it still pains me that my children continue to hold onto the tumultuous memories of their parents' marriage to this day. Unfortunately, we made it about us, and thus took our eyes off of the prize during our heated arguments and selfish ways. To my children, I say this: It is my sincere prayer that your parents' immaturity will make you better parents and better human beings.

I am also thankful to my editor for her patience and valuable suggestions, as well as my illustrator, who, with her creative hand, perfectly captured the emotional dialogue of Growing Up Like Joseph in a relevant and meaningful way.

Lastly, to my dear mother—I miss you every day!

Please chalk it up to my head and not my heart if I forgot anyone!

About the Author

Nadirah Maryam Muhammad is a licensed marriage and family therapist associate and, most importantly, a mother of three. She practices collaborative therapy out of Houston, Texas, and has been dedicated to providing marriage, parenting, and relationship counseling to those in need since 1996. Aside from therapy, she is also an adjunct psychology professor and currently in pursuit of her Ph. D in The Psychology of Business from The Chicago School of Professional Psychology. Her two previous degrees come from the esteemed Prairie View A&M University.

When not working or studying the latest in psychology, she enjoys spending time with her family and practicing her faith, as well as sewing, canning, reading, playing the piano, and listening to her favorite music – classic oldies.

Joseph stood with his class on the auditorium stage. His head hung low as if trying to hide.

He wouldn't make eye contact with anyone. He didn't realize that his actions made him very noticeable.

He fought the tears back until the school concert was over. As he rushed off stage, the waterworks came.

Joseph wiped his tears and pressed his chin as far into his chest as he could. "I miss Dad," he mumbled.

"What did you say?" said Mom. "I can't hear you. Stop crying!"

"I don't know," is all Joseph could say. Then he whispered, "I want Dad to come back."

With his chin still in his chest, Joseph looked up. The other kids and parents were exiting the auditorium and staring as they walked past.

"Joseph," said Mom, "if you want, we can call your dad now."

Joseph stared back at the floor.
"No, I'll go to class."

He dried his eyes and walked down the hall.

After school, Joseph rode the bus home with his younger brother.

Joseph was silent.

When the boys got home, their grandmother was waiting for them. "How was your day?"

"It was good, G," said Matthew.

Joseph was silent.

"Okay, boys, get your book bags and start your homework."

Joseph plopped on the couch and finally broke his silence. "I don't want to. I'll do it later."

"No Joseph. While I cook dinner you'll do your homework," said G. "Let's get it out of the way now."

Joseph stood up and rolled his eyes.

"No. I'll do it later."

G's face grew stern. "Joseph, did you just roll your eyes? Are you talking back to me?

Just get your books."

"AHHHHHHH." Tears began to stream down Joseph's face. "I can't take it. I always have to do things I don't want to." He stopped to gasp for air then cried hysterically.

Matthew went to his brother. "What's the matter?"

"SHUT UP! Get away from me," screamed Joseph.

G took Joseph in her arms and hugged him.

"It's okay, sweetie. It's okay."

When Mom got home, Joseph could hear his mom and grandmother whispering.

After dinner, Mom sat with Joseph. "I know you're having trouble dealing with your father leaving. I'm having a hard time too.

"I think it's time we get some help. I'm going to talk to the school counselor and find a child therapist, someone we can both talk to. Matthew, too."

Joseph's eyes became watery.
"Can we ask Dad to come?"

"I don't know," said Mom.
"What if he says, no.
How will that make us feel?"

Joseph stood up and wiped his eyes. "I guess you're right. I just feel safer when he's around."

He shoved his hands in his pockets and went to his room.

The next day at school, Joseph's teacher called him to her desk. "Joseph, your mom called this morning. You have an appointment with Mr. Gonzalez, the school guidance counselor. He's in room 305."

Joseph sat and looked around the room, avoiding eye contact with the counselor.

"How about I start," said Mr. Gonzalez. "You feel miserable. There's something wrong and you can't put your finger on it. Am I close?"

"I see," said Mr. Gonzalez. "Why do you think this is happening?"

Joseph looked at the floor. "I guess because my father moved out a couple of months ago. It stinks. I feel . . . I feel like the floor opened up and swallowed me. Sometimes I feel like I can't breathe."

Mr. Gonzalez handed Joseph a pamphlet.

"You can read this at home. One of the first things you can do to help yourself is to talk about your feelings.

"You can talk to your mom or other family members. You'll be talking to me too.

And, I spoke with your mom this morning; she's making an appointment with a great therapist I recommended."

Joseph looked at the pamphlet. "Drawing, sports, breathing. I do all that stuff."

"Well," said Mr. Gonzalez as he got up. "It means become occupied with something when you're feeling overwhelmed. Take your mind off of the bad and on to something good."

Mr. Gonzalez put his hand on Joseph's shoulder. "And, the breathing is deep breathing. It really helps calm you down."

The counselor walked Joseph to the door. "I'll see you tomorrow. In the meantime, try some of the tips in the pamphlet."

As Joseph left he felt a bit better. *He's not bad,* he thought.

I think he's someone I can talk to.

When Joseph and Matthew got home, G was starting dinner. "How was your day?"

"Great," said Matthew. "I got a 95 on my math test."

Joseph rolled his eyes and dropped his book bag on the floor. "I did my homework in school. I'm going to my room to read."

G let him be.

"Joseph," called mom. "Come eat."

Joseph shoved the pamphlet in his back pocket and went to the kitchen.

"How was your day?" asked mom. "Did you like Mr. Gonzalez?"

"It was okay," said Joseph. "And, he's okay. He gave me something to read."

Mom smiled. "I know, he left me a pamphlet at the school office. I picked it up on the way home. Maybe we can go over it later, together.

I think Matthew should be in on it too."

After dinner, Mom, Joseph, and Matthew sat around the kitchen table.

"Boys," said Mom, "I know it's tough without Dad here. Do you have any questions about what's going on?"

Joseph got up and paced the floor. "Yeah, I have questions. Will we be able to stay here?

Will you have to get a second job? Will G be moving in with us? Does Dad even want to see us?"

Matthew just listened and watched.

"Honey," said Mom. "Those are all good questions, but I don't have all the answers just yet. I want you to know though that none of this was your fault or Matthew's. Sometimes people just grow apart."

Matthew's face dropped and his eyes teared up. "Will you grow apart from me and Joseph? Will you leave us?"

Joseph put his arm around his little brother. "One thing I know, little bro, Mom will never leave us. And, I'll never leave you."

Mom got up and hugged her boys. "Thank you for helping, Joseph. I made an appointment with a Mrs. Keys. She's a child therapist. We'll go as a family to work through all our feelings and questions. Dad is even willing to attend sessions with us if it will help you."

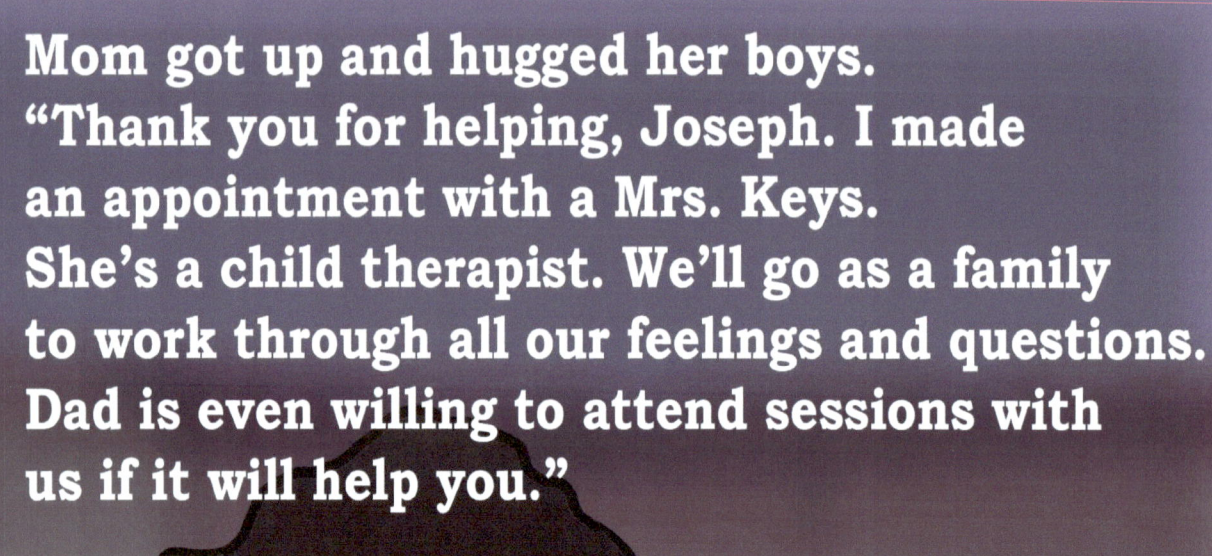

Mom squeezed her boys even tighter. "I know we'll be just fine."

www.ingramcontent.com/pod-product-compliance
Lightning Source LLC
LaVergne TN
LVHW072056070426
835508LV00002B/127